UNMASKED

Walking Out Of The Shadows Of Your Past

Charles J. Bennett III

CJC PUBLISHING COMPANY
EL PASO, TEXAS

Unmasked

Walking Out Of The Shadows Of Your Past

CJC PUBLISHING COMPANY
1208 Sumac Drive
El Paso, TX 79925

Printed in the United States of America
Library of Congress Control Number: 2011932232
ISBN: 1-930388-89-6

Edited by Delgar Publishing

Editorial assistance by Talisha L. Bennett & Caryn C. Newman

Cover design by Charles J. Bennett III

Published by CJC Publishing Company

Unless otherwise stated, all Scripture quotations are from the King James Version.

Table Contents

Acknowledgement

I would like to first thank my wonderful wife Talisha, for all of your continuos love, support and encouragement. You are my best friend in the world and I appreciate you very much. To my children, Charles IV, Adria, Cyesha, and Cya, thank you for loving me unconditionally. It is my desire to leave a legacy for you.

To my parents Charles, Debra and Valerie, my brother Isaiah, sisters Sharise, Bertha, and Nadriah and to my family I love you all very much.

To my mentor/pastor/father and mother Dr. Mikel and Debra Brown, thank you for seeing in me what I could not see in myself. Thank you for never giving up on me.

To Gary Sparkman, the author of ***Dare to Discover Yourself*** for your words of encouragement and enlightenment through this process.

To my CJC family, you have seen me grow, and laughed with and at me all the way. I Love you all dearly.

My Alamogordo family, I love you dearly, I have learned just as much from you then you have learn from me. I just pray that I have impacted and made a difference in your life in someway. I endeavor to be an example of faithfulness and loyalty before you in all I do.

Preface

If you do not conquer yourself, you will be conquered by self.
- Napoleon Hill

Most of the enemies of our progress and success are unseen. They are imbedded in our excuses and entrenched in our fears. They are the unseen battles that we all encounter when we are all alone and have to face ourselves.

We use many excuses to justify inactivity or our failure to start a journey. Excuses are simply extended lies we tell ourselves to cover up the insecurities, inadequacies and any other such things in our lives that we just do not want to face.

However, be encouraged. You are so close to turning everything in your life around. You are just one decision away from the total life make-over you desire.

In order to experience the substantive change you desire, you must be prepared to do certain things you have never done before. You must brave the unknown along roads you have never traveled before.

Along the way, you will indeed face your deepest fears and confront your own destructive tendencies that have always surfaced to undermine your present progress and erase future hope.

As my mentor often says, "You are your greatest asset." Conversely, we can also be our greatest liability, as well.

The secret unseen internal struggles that we face can potentially be the greatest hindrance to our progress in life. It is not the external challenges you encounter that will prove to be your greatest opponent. Instead, it is that internal adversary—those proverbial "demons" within—that time and again prove to be the cause of our undoing and the biggest impediments to our achieving anything worthwhile.

You and I are going to live in our tomorrows. So, why not live in the ones of our choosing.

CHAPTER 1

Conquering Yourself

CHAPTER 1

Conquering Yourself

Make no mistake... The greatest battle you will ever fight will not be fought on external soil. Conflict with a spouse, a parent, a sibling, or a neighbor cannot compare to the magnitude of the ultimate struggle you will be required to overcome in order to achieve greatness. The brief skirmishes on your job between you and a co-worker also pale in comparison. On the contrary, your greatest battle will be fought on internal soil—that of the heart and mind. Thus, your greatest battle boils down to a defining struggle between the person you currently are and the individual you desire to become.

Inside every person who aspires to higher heights and greater possibilities in life is an enemy who does not want to take that journey. Our challenge, therefore, is to conquer that vagrant who wants nothing more than a free ride through life. The war that perhaps wages inside you at this very moment is an actual conflict between the champion you were born to be and the under-achiever who was created by life's disappointments and misfortunes.

However, there is good news for those individuals who persevere and overcome their internal enemies. The abundant spoils of victory acquired in battle will not only serve you well in this lifetime, but they will also accrue to the estate of your good works to endure throughout eternity. After you have gained the upper hand over the enemy within, you will then reap the priceless fruit of victory that will enable you to feed and impact countless lives for years to come.

In the book of Proverbs, Solomon provides us with some very sobering wisdom:

> It is better to be patient than powerful. It is better to win control over yourself than over whole cities.
>
> Proverbs 16:32 (GNT)

You must learn to conquer the very things that threaten your purpose and dreams. You must gain victory over those destructive habits that threaten your destiny, both present and future. Keep in mind that many people are connected to your success, and they are therefore dependent upon you remaining faithful to the great mandate on your life. What you achieve in life affects more than just you. What good is it to win an actual physical battle but lose the overall war by surrendering precious ground to your own sexual lust, anger, low self-esteem, and unforgiveness. What profit is there in conquering one's enemies and then losing the internal struggles? Such imbalance yields very little fruit.

You must learn to conquer the very things that threaten your purpose and dreams.

In writing to young Timothy, the Apostle Paul encouraged him by declaring:

> For physical training is of some value (useful for a little), but godliness (spiritual training) is useful and of value in everything and in every way, for it holds promise for the present life and also for the life which is to come.
>
> 1 Timothy 4:8 (AMP)

My strength is not measured by how many victories I can accumulate over another. My strength is not calculated by the degree to which I can control another. My strength is not gauged by how much weight I can lift. My strength is not scored by how I govern myself in front of others. My strength is not revealed in how I deal with external battles. Rather, it is displayed by how well I deal with my internal challenges.

Why is this so true? It is true because our internal battles cut deeper and their wounds fester longer than wounds to the physical body. In all actuality, we are all far more likely to recover quicker and more thoroughly from our flesh wounds than from any emotional scars we will ever sustain in life.

I just have to FACE it! I must face the challenge head on. Walking by faith for believers does not mean that we live in a constant state of denial. Yet, I believe most Christians see living by faith to mean just that. If I fail to face situations that exist in front of me, they are only going to get worse. Ignoring them will not cause them to disappear. Situations seldom get better when left to chance. I must boldly face that which threatens my purpose and destiny. I must also find the courage to identify and address those harmful aspects of my past that continue to both wreak havoc on my present, and also siphon off potential from my future. I cannot afford to simply sit back and wait for the cavalry to come and rescue me. I hate to be the bearer of bad news...but the cavalry is not coming, and that star you've been wishing on is never going to appear. You must face your situations and summon the courage to make the necessary course corrections to improve your circumstances.

The majority of the things we experience in our present are as a direct result of past bad decision making. Many of our problems are self-induced. We are the source of most of our problems, and the great news is that we are also the solution to our problems. We must take responsibility for the current conditions of our lives. Owning up to our past failures does not mean that we allow them to become crutches or excuses. What it does mean is that I now take responsibility, so I can exercise authority over the affairs of my life.

Owning up to our past failures does not mean that we allow them to become crutches or excuses.

When I pass the blame or responsibility, I also pass along to another the power and authority to make whatever changes I deemed are necessary. When God created the earth and everything in it, He gave the responsibility and authority for its care to Adam and his wife, Eve. He gave them the power to dominate and control everything on the earth, including Satan himself. In the book of Genesis, God declared:

> Then God said, "Let us make man in our image, in our likeness, and let them rule over the fish of the sea and the birds of the air, over the livestock, over all the earth, and over all the creatures that move along the ground."
>
> Genesis 1:26 (NIV)

God placed all of the power in their hands. They were considered the responsible ones. So it is with mankind today. We have the ability to shape our own world. The change we desire to see in our lives is within our power to bring about. But just as it was with the first man and woman who made bad decisions and then tried to shirk responsibility, authority and control also get taken and then passed along to someone else. The first accounts of man's transgressions in the Garden of Eden reveal man's tendency to pass along responsibility, as well as the authority that goes with it:

> And he said, "Who told you that you were naked? Have you eaten from the tree that commanded you not to eat from?" The man said, "The woman you put here with me—she gave me some fruit from the tree, and I ate it." Then the LORD God said to the woman, "What is this you have done?"

> The woman said, "The serpent deceived me, and I ate."
>
> Genesis 3:11-13 (NIV)

It is important to note that whoever bears the responsibility also possesses the authority to make the necessary changes. Adam blamed Eve, Eve blamed the serpent, and neither of them had the courage to face and own up to what they had done. The power and control was in their hand, but when they placed the blame or responsibility on the serpent, they also relinquished their control and shifted the balance of power to him as well. If you want to take back the authority in your life, then stand up and take responsibility for your current situation. Then you will have the power to chart a new destination for your future.

Whoever bears the responsibility also possesses the authority to make the necessary changes.

We must learn to conquer our deepest fears. Our lustful passions are not just confined to sensual desires, but they encompass all of our desires to do things outside of the plan that God has for us. We must gain victory over our unforgiveness, offenses committed against others, and apathy. You can conquer what has been conquering you. You have the ability to render the negative things in your life helpless by the power of the Spirit of God. The Apostle Paul said it this way when writing to the Christians in Rome:

> For if you live according to the sinful nature, you will die; but if by the Spirit you put to death the misdeeds of the body, you will live.
>
> Romans 8:13 (NIV)

There is no temptation or challenge you will ever face that you do not have the power within you to overcome. When writing to encourage Believers in the Greek city-state of Corinth, Paul writes:

> No temptation has overtaken you except such as is common to man; but God is faithful, who will not allow you to be tempted beyond what you are able, but with the temptation will also make the way of escape, that you may be able to bear it.
>
> 1 Corinthians 10:13 (NKJV)

Jesus Christ, the greatest example for any man to follow, had to deal with this very thing in the Garden of Gethsemane. Jesus' greatest battle was not external. There was a storm that arose while He and His disciples were traveling to Capernaum. The wind raged and the sea tossed boisterously. This caused great fear to arise in the heart of his followers—so much so that they woke Jesus from His sleep and asked Him if He cared whether or not they perished.

Now let us examine how Jesus responded to their fears and concerns in this situation.

> Jesus was sleeping at the back of the boat with his head on a cushion. The disciples woke him up, shouting, "Teacher, don't you care that we're going to drown?" When Jesus woke up, he rebuked the wind and said to the waves, "Silence! Be still!" Suddenly the wind stopped, and there was a great calm. Then he asked them, "Why are you afraid? Do you still have no faith?"
>
> Mark 4:38-40 (NLT)

The first thing we must notice is that during this storm Jesus is asleep. This should suggest to us that Jesus was able to maintain an internal peace; although, He was surrounded by an external storm. His peace was so complete that the chaos surrounding Him never disturbed Him, and through it all, He maintained a posture of calm and rest.

Secondly, we need to examine His actions after the disciples disturbed His rest. After He was awakened, Jesus first calmly spoke to the wind, and then he commanded the natural elements by simply declaring, "peace be still." Notice that He first spoke to the unseen wind. Then He spoke to that which was visible, namely the waves.

From this illustration, we can see the powerful influence that unseen forces can exert on those things we are able to see around us everyday. Notice that Jesus spoke to His external environment so that it would mirror his internal environment, which was one of PEACE. This is a lesson we need to keep in mind. If we would first deal with the internal issues of life, then the external issues would have to fall in line, accordingly.

From this story, we see that our greatest battles in life are not as a result of those great disturbances around us. In fact, Jesus was not unsettled when He had to feed a multitude of people with a few fish and a few loaves of bread. Furthermore, His encounters with demonic principalities did nothing to cause Him to deviate from His mission on earth. Instead, it only furthered it. On the other hand, however...

Jesus' greatest battle took place when He was all alone in the Garden of Gethsemane. It was in the garden, for the very first time, that Jesus agonized over what He wanted to do versus what He was sent to earth by God to do. His agonies did not stem from the winds, waves, feeding hungry people, or His confrontations with demons. Alone in the garden, He battled within himself against a desire to follow two destinies—one of God's design and the other of His own making.

In essence, he had to conquer himself. He had to deal with the fact that he was sent to earth for the express purpose of being beaten, being hung on the cross, and going to hell in our stead. Now let me be very clear here, Jesus did not agonize out of fear of any of these things. The thing that concerned him most was the separation from the Father he would experience for the first time once he took upon himself the sin of the world. In this great struggle, we witness how Jesus confronted his greatest challenge...that war that raged within him.

You and I are not exempt from such internal struggle. We will face our own great challenges, as well. The Apostle Paul, who was a premier teacher in his time and a man who wrote two-thirds of the New Testament, experienced a battle far greater than any religious system of that day. His greatest opposition was not the Herodians, the Judaizers, the various Jewish religious sects, or the many unbelievers he encountered on his missionary journeys.

Paul's biggest struggle occurred when he had to

deal with the thorn in his flesh. He himself said that he asked God three times to remove it. Having to conquer his own flesh would prove more daunting a task than the many enemies he would face taking the Gospel all over Asia Minor. Paul found that it was far more difficult to conquer his own internal issues.

Paul provides us with a hint of the nature of his inner wrestling:

> To keep me from becoming conceited because of these surpassingly great revelations, there was given me a thorn in my flesh, a messenger of Satan, to torment me. Three times I pleaded with the Lord to take it away from me. But he said to me, "My grace is sufficient for you, for my power is made perfect in weakness." Therefore I will boast all the more gladly about my weaknesses, so that Christ's power may rest on me.
>
> 2 Corinthians 12:7-9 (NIV)

Understand that we must all deal first with ourselves. We are triune beings just like God. I am not speaking here about the fact that I am body, soul, and spirit. No, I am talking about the other trinity. The Three P's that comprise who I am:

Three P's are:

1. The Public ME – This is the image I portray to the world, the ME I am in front of people. This is the person I want people to think I am. The Public Me is the mask I put on in order to communicate and interact with others in society.

2. The Perceived ME – This is the person people think I am. Although people are going to make their assessments about who I am and what I possess anyway, this particular image and opinion of me is, in many cases, influenced to a great extent by my public persona. The Perceived ME is how the people that I deal with on a daily basis see me.
AND then you have…

3. The Private ME –This is who I really am. This is the real me, apart from all of the things that I use to define me. This is me, without titles, degrees, or positions. This is the real me without all of the accolades and accomplishments I use as make-up to cover over my issues and flaws.

The first two identities are the areas people spend the majority of their time and resources trying to fix up. We try to apply bandages to areas of our lives that are actually in need of major surgery. We tend to deal only with the symptoms and never with the root causes of our problems.

In his first epistle to Timothy, Paul writes:

> For physical training is of some value, but godliness has value for all things, holding promise for both the present life and the life to come.
>
> 1 Timothy 4:8 (NIV)

The scripture does not teach that dealing with the external aspects of our lives does not profit us or that we should ignore our physical appearance. No! Instead, the scriptures help us to prioritize. The writer here is helping us to see that all of the focus should not be placed on the external, but that the focus should first and foremost be placed on the internal matters of our lives. If we do not deal with the third and most important ME, then the Public and Perceived ME will fall apart right before our eyes. Then the only one who will be left in public shame will be the Private ME, the real me, uncovered and completely exposed for the entire world to see.

The Gospel of Luke reveals a very sobering truth regarding living one way in public and another way behind closed doors:

> There is nothing concealed that will not be disclosed, or hidden that will not be made known. What you have said in the dark will

> be heard in the daylight, and what you have whispered in the ear in the inner rooms will be proclaimed from the roofs.
>
> Luke 12:2-3 (NIV)

Why expose it? Because if I expose it, I control with whom I share the information, preferably with a qualified source. Additionally, I control in which environment the information is revealed.

There have been many prominent Church leaders who have suffered tremendous humiliation behind the public exposure of their secret sins. I firmly believe that, in all such cases, at some point God convicts the heart and sends clear warnings to provide the individuals an opportunity to deal privately with their sin issues. However, God is forced to pull back the curtain on our closet sins when we fail to heed His warnings. Then we are left to deal with the full weight of public scrutiny and ridicule. So, if we deal with problem areas in our lives and expose them ourselves when we are convicted by God, then we avoid having to face the embarrassment of public exposure over issues that should have be dealt with privately. Open and public shame is the result when we attempt to live behind masks of untruth.

In Act 1, scene 3 of William Shakespeare's famous play, ***Hamlet***, Polonius imparts a last bit of advice to his son Laertes in saying, "This above all: to thine own self be true..."

In writing to the Christians in the Church of Corinth, Paul said it this way:

> Stop deceiving yourselves.
> 1 Corinthians 3:18 (NLT)

In all honesty, most people live their lives as though they are Shakespearean actors, going from one character to the next and from one scene to another—never really being true to self. We put on our masks and try our best to assume the role that best serves the audience before us.

But... Will the real (insert your name here) please stand up!

CHAPTER 2

The Masquerade

CHAPTER

The Masquerade

When the lights come on, it's time to perform. The camera is rolling; you have to put on a good show. A-n-n-d action! It's time to put on a happy face, as the song would say. It's time to put on my mask and to pretend that all is well; even though, I know it is not. Who am I really? Because I have acted for so long, the real me tends to get lost somewhere between all of the performances, and I'm not even an actor.

No... Truth be told, I am an actor. The difference with me is that I'm not getting paid for the work I put in. Who am I? I can give you the textbook answer, or I can offer you society's definition of me. But after everything is said and done, the real question is...What do I believe in my heart concerning my true identity? Well, if you examine my life and listen closely to what I say, eventually my speech, decisions, and actions will betray my pretenses. Careful scrutiny will expose the real me and even pinpoint what I really believe about myself—someone who is in fact vastly different from the public perception.

It is very difficult to maintain any masquerade for an extended amount of time. Eventually cracks appear and leaks begin to develop beneath the surface of any façade or fake front. At some point we eventually get tired of acting and looking like someone we are not. It's like being an undercover cop on a never-ending assignment. And when you least expect it, you lower your guard and the real you and the pretend you begin reading the scripts to the wrong movies. Your pretend character is suddenly at a loss in the world of reality, while your true character is like a fish out of water in the land of make-believe. Such is the inevitable confusion that arises when we try to live double lives.

So the question then is, how do I get from where I currently am to where I desire to be? I discovered long ago that the same information controlling my thoughts also determines my belief system. It matters not whether the information is true or false. Given enough time, it will eventually become my truth and reality.

Reality is based on perception. It follows then that my perception is determined by the information I take in. Let me clarify that. It is determined by the information I become intimate with. If I never embrace and become intimate with the information I take in, I will never become persuaded by it. Once persuaded, however, a certain confidence begins to take hold, which then displaces fears that used to exist. But...fear of what? The fear of being me and worrying about what others may say, think, or what I perceive they will think.

Reality is based on perception.

When a manufacturer creates a product, he first determines the product's function and purpose. The product does not assign purpose and function to itself. Moreover, the creation can never find fulfillment in doing anything other than what it was created to do. Furthermore, the manufacturer or creator will never receive accolades or praise if the product does not function in the way it was designed. Therefore, my fulfillment in life is imbedded within my purpose for being on this planet. You and I were created for a particular purpose; although, we may be able to do many different things. We must go to the creator to find out the purpose of our existence. Then and only then will we know who we really are?

I have learned that despite how much my parents, mentors, pastor, and even God Himself want me to succeed in life, they cannot cause me to succeed. This does not suggest that God lacks anything or that the others do not influence my life. But the bottom-line is that the power to succeed has been placed in my hands. No one can make me believe what God has said about me. My mother told me one day standing outside of the church, "I can't want more for you than you want for yourself." Even though she loves me and wants the best for me, not even she can bring about my success. Joshua 1:8 declares, "I make my way prosperous". Success is a choice...it is my choice.

> *"Nothing can stop the man with the right mental attitude from achieving his goal; nothing on earth can help the man with the wrong mental attitude."*
>
> - Thomas Jefferson

A well-known author and public speaker made a statement that really brought this point home for me.

He said:

"I wish I could tell you that if you had a great father, one who loves you, who is successful and nurtures you that this would ensure your success. I can't because that's not the truth. Solomon and Absalom both had the same father, King David. Solomon became a very wealthy and wise man while Absalom tried to take his father's kingdom and ultimately died at the hand of his father's soldiers."

He went on to say:

"I wish I could tell you that if you had a great mentor, one who could see your potential, speak into your life and help to eliminate your flaws that this would ensure your success. I can't, because that's not true either. Peter and Judas both had Jesus. Peter went on to head the church in Jerusalem and preached such a powerful message that 3000 people were saved in one day, but Judas, on the other hand, betrayed Jesus and committed suicide."

Your mentor is not the one who gives you the instruction you need. He or she is the one whose instructions you take and apply to your life.

Contrary to what people may think, your mentor is not the one who gives you the instruction you need. He or she is the one whose instructions you take and apply to your life.

There is something that my pastor once said to me that greatly troubled me. He said, "Charles..." When he called me Charles I knew it was serious because he rarely addresses me by my first name. He said, "If you do not learn to overcome some things in your life, you will never be who God has purposed you to be." His statement troubled me because I thought that the person God had purposed me to be and what he designed for me to do would ultimately come to pass regardless of my actions. I thought that God was in control and that all I had to do was sit back, put my life in neutral, and simply allow God to wake me up when I reached my destination.

My purpose, my dream, or what God has shown me, is what he desires for me. I have the potential of seeing these things come to pass, but if I do not fight for my dream, protect my purpose and go through the qualifying process to attain them, it all remains just that—a mere dream, never to become my reality. I found that reading the Word of God, hearing it, and quoting it is good, but none of those things will impress God or lead me to my purpose. But what will impress God and bring about change in my life is my decision to believe what He desires for me and then acting on what I have chosen to believe.

> Your word I have hidden in my heart, That I might not sin against You
>
> Psalm 119:11 (NKJV)

The scripture does not say that I will not sin against God. Indeed, I will sin against God if I do not apply or obey the Word that I choose to hide in my heart. Now don't get me wrong, knowing the word of God is vital to your success, but simply having God's truth does not ensure success. The outcome is still up to you. Hiding the Word in my heart does not ensure I will not transgress the law of God. It simply means that the more Word of God that I hide in my heart greatly increases the possibility that I will not sin against Him. If I choose to put the word of God and the principles I have learned into operation, then these things and many others will help me succeed in every area of my life.

I remember working on my first CD. I was excited about seeing the finished project. I put in the time to produce, write and record the music. I also invested money into the mastering and printing of the disc. I was so happy that I accomplished one of my dreams. But because of what I thought about myself, I did not push my dream like I should or could have. How do you sale someone on something you do not believe in yourself? In this case, it should have been very easy since it was my dream, after all. I had to later admit to my wife, who by the way supported and helped finance the project, that I did not promote it because I didn't think it was good enough. Not just the music or the project, but me.

For many of us, from a very young age, we have been categorized and compared with our siblings, cousins and childhood friends so often that we never have a chance to discover who we truly are. The real you gets buried almost immediately. With the many frequent and drastic public image changes we undergo early in life, it is virtually impossible to keep up with the many different faces we must wear in front of family, friends, and co-workers. So you go through life conforming to what others deem as acceptable, leaving you unhappy, unsatisfied, and unfulfilled.

There is a disease that has and is affecting many people all over the world. It has spread from generation to generation. This disease or dis-ease knows no race, color, or sex. The prefix "dis" means to deprive of or to have a negative, or reversing force. The root word "ease" means the state of being comfortable or freedom from constraint and discomfort. The disease I am referring to is Comparisonitis. Comparisonitis negatively affects the mentality of the infected individual. Through the infected mentality the disease flows through the individual, affecting all potential productivity in every area of the person's life. This disease causes you to compare yourself to others. As a result, you will experience feelings of inadequacy and or a profound sense of insecurity. This disease causes an individual to be deprived of the comfort and freedom of being themselves.

In Dr. Mikel Brown's book ***Beyond Ordinary,*** he says, "if you compare you compete." Also, when you compare, you become discontented. You become so overwhelmed with what you perceive another person to possess that you lose sight of or devalue what you have. This is the challenge that many people face.

I discovered that most of my feelings of inadequacy were birthed from comparisonitis. I would secretly compare myself with someone else, or I would try to impress people so they would think highly of me; although, the individuals would be totally unaware of my secret competition with them. If anyone had examined my actions closely, they would have been tipped off to my charade by the results my life was producing.

There was a woman in the Bible whose husband died unexpectedly—unexpectedly because he didn't have time to put his financial affairs in order before leaving the scene. He left her with many debts to pay, and the bill collectors were threatening to take her sons in order to satisfy his debt obligations. So, she went to the prophet (the individual whom her husband had served faithfully) seeking help. Well, the prophet asked her a simple question.

> So Elisha said to her, "What shall I do for you? Tell me, what do you have in the house?" And she said, "Your maidservant has nothing in the house but a jar of oil."
>
> 2 Kings 4:2 (NKJV)

The house does not just include the physical house, but the question extends to include the person's entire being. So, what do you have inside you that can perhaps turn around your current situation? Her reply to the prophet then is just like many replies today. "Your maidservant has nothing" or in other words, I have nothing in me that can change my situation. She went to the prophet hoping he would do it for her. She believed she had nothing. When she finally recognized that she did have something, notice how she described it..."but a jar of oil" or, in others words, oh by the way I have a jar of oil. She totally underestimated the value of what she had in her possession. But it was that very thing that was instrumental in turning things around for her.

In my church, we have very talented musicians. I found myself secretly comparing my music abilities with theirs, and in my assessment, my talent did not measure up to theirs. It did not matter that countless people had told me they love my music and that it truly blesses them. I only concluded that what I had to offer the world was not good enough. Consequently, I unwittingly sabotaged my own success, as my mentor would say. I slammed on the breaks and stopped the progress I was making all because of how I viewed myself and how I valued the gifts that God had given to me.

I believe it is very difficult to assess your self worth correctly without knowing who you are. The fear of success can be just as crippling as the fear of failure. If all I've experienced in life is failure, how can I truly prepare to succeed? What if I do win, how do I respond? What if my dreams do become a reality, what do I do then? Just as many people have been destroyed by success as by failure. Therefore, despite the success or failure that will inevitably come my way, I must know for certain who I am, and I must be fully persuaded that I am good enough.

It is very difficult to assess yourself worth correctly without knowing who you are.

We must stop trying to impress other individuals because people are very fickle; their opinions shift like sand on a beach. One day they will love you and the next day they will hate you. If anyone knows how unstable public opinions are, Jesus certainly does. In the eleventh chapter of the book of Mark, we witness a great outpouring of support and appreciation for Jesus. Then we see a rapid shift in the popular sentiment regarding Jesus and his ministry:

> And they that went before, and they that followed, cried, saying, Hosanna; Blessed is he that cometh in the name of the Lord: Blessed be the kingdom of our father David, that cometh in the name of the Lord: Hosanna in the highest.
>
> Mark 11:9-10 (KJV)

By the time we catch up with Jesus again in the fifteenth chapter of Mark, the public sentiment by the same crowd of people has changed very dramatically:

> And they cried out again, Crucify him. Then Pilate said unto them, Why, what evil hath he done? And they cried out the more exceedingly, Crucify him.
>
> Mark 15:13-14 (KJV)

This goes to show that people's opinions of you can change with the wind. Therefore, you cannot afford to allow their opinions to shape your view of yourself. As a former Airman, I recall vividly, while stationed in Okinawa, Japan, first learning about currency exchange rates. At the time, I had no idea that the value of the dollar fluctuated on a daily basis in comparison to other world currencies. Being stationed overseas, to us military personnel, the 1st and 15th of each month took on a whole new significance because the value of the dollar on those particular days would determine how much we would get paid. And similar to those constantly floating monetary exchange rates, my self-worth continued to fluctuate, as long as I lived based upon the opinions of others.

But I learned that it is not in my best interest to peg my worth to anything that is subject to the whims of change. I determined that I must allow God's view of me to shape not only my self-worth but also my self-esteem because God never changes.

> Malachi 3:6 (NIV) states, "I the LORD do not change."

The same way He felt about me in the beginning is the same way He feels about me now, despite the many mistakes I've made over the years. I am still valuable to God.

> Luke 12:7 declares, "But even the very hairs of your head are all numbered. Fear not therefore: ye are of more value than many sparrows."

God values me and He showed it by giving the greatest gift He could give, His son Jesus. The scriptures spell out God's love for me in John 3:16 (NIV) by declaring,"For God so loved the world that he gave his one and only Son, that whoever believes in him shall not perish but have eternal life." I may not have been worthy of that gift, but no doubt I must have been worth the expense and investment of God sending His only begotten son to save a wretch like me. Therefore, I must constantly think of myself the way God thinks of me because His thoughts are consistent and always good. Whenever you are in doubt as to your worth in God's plan, remember...

> I know what I'm doing. I have it all planned out—plans to take care of you, not abandon you, plans to give you the future you hope for.
>
> Jeremiah 29:11 (MSG)

This brings me to the conclusion. You should be at a point where you can now begin to believe that you are good enough and that you no longer need to pretend to be anyone else. The world needs to meet the real you. God knew what He was doing when He formed you in your mother's womb, but now you must pursue the plan He has for you in the earth. We're waiting!

CHAPTER 3

A Change of Heart

CHAPTER 3

A Change of Heart

Henry Ford, founder of the Ford Motor Company, once said, "The man who thinks he can and the man who thinks he can't are both right." What makes this statement true? The truth is found in the fact that one's actions are determined by what he or she thinks and comes to believe.

> Proverbs 23:7 says, "As a man thinks in his heart, so is he."

This passage is not suggesting that we will magically turn into whatever we are thinking about at the moment. Rather, the passage suggests that, over time, individuals come to behave in a manner consistent with their dominant beliefs.

The information you receive is what affects your decision-making, which determines your actions and ultimately the entire course of your life.

In order to change the direction of your life, you must change your actions. In order to change your actions, you must change your decisions. In order to change your decisions, you must change the way you think. And in order to change the way you think, you must change the information you receive. PLAIN and SIMPLE!

Believe it or not, we are the sum total of the information we receive on a daily basis. If you were to inventory the vast amount of information you take in daily, you would discover a clear path leading from the accumulation of information in your mind to the very bedrock of your belief system. The information you receive is what affects your decision-making, which determines your actions and ultimately the entire course of your life.

It is not good enough to just get information; you must insure that you get the right information. Then, you must choose to believe and act on the information you receive in order to reprogram your thinking or thought patterns. Proverbs often refers to this central place of activity as the "heart."

The Strong's Concordance defines it this way…"the heart is the middle, central or innermost part of man. His soul or mind, as it is the seat of the thoughts, passions, desires, appetites, affections, purpose and endeavors. It is the seat of his understanding, faculty, intelligence, will and character." The heart is so important that God tells us to Guard our heart (mind, will, seat of appetites, desires, passions and emotions) above all else, for it determines the course of your life (Proverbs 4:23 NLT). The words "above all else" are used to convey the importance of guarding the heart. We must learn to protect our hearts because out of it (the heart) flows the source (issues) of everything we do and speak, which, in a nutshell, boils down to the entire life of an individual.

There is an old expression that says "you are what you eat." This expression suggests that whatever you consume will make up your body's composition. If you indulge in unhealthy eating, the result will be an unhealthy body. The expression also suggests that only what goes in me is the substance or material that can come out of me.

Luke 6:45 (NIV) says it this way:

> The good man brings good things out of the good stored up in his heart, and the evil man brings evil things out of the evil stored

> up in his heart. For out of the overflow of his heart his mouth speaks.

The scriptures here suggest that what we allow to be stored in our heart will dictate what we speak and what we do. In this passage, we see that the good man does good things and the evil man does evil things because of what is stored in their respective hearts. In the book of Matthew, Jesus shares the same truth in this manner:

> But what comes out of the mouth gets its start in the heart. It's from the heart that we vomit up evil arguments, murders, adulteries, fornications, thefts, lies, and cussing.
>
> Matthew 15:18-19 (MSG)

It all starts in the heart. I must begin to change my heart or guard what I allow to be stored in it. Therefore, it's not just what I think that makes the difference. Rather, it is what I believe in my heart that makes all the difference.

If what you say you believe and the results you are getting are not in agreement, then there is a problem. The problem may not be what you are saying or hearing; it may be that you don't fully believe what you are confessing. The results of what I say are demonstrative of my belief. I will not get the result of what I say. I will, however, get the result of what I believe in my heart and then say with my mouth.

The secret is in my believing—what I believe in my heart.

> Mark 11:23 (NIV) says, "I tell you the truth, if anyone says to this mountain, 'Go, throw yourself into the sea,' and does not doubt in his heart but believes (believe where, in his heart) that what he says will happen, it will be done for him."

It is difficult to consistently declare what I do not really believe. What a person truly believes is revealed in those casual moments, when their guard is down and the words come tumbling forth.

A person's true beliefs are not typically revealed while at church, in the presence of fellow Christians because at those times, our guard is up. In such familiar settings, we all know the proper lingo and the right things to say. On the other hand, what I truly believe is often displayed when I am at home or around people with whom I am comfortable.

I can recall a particular instance when I was standing in front of the church, simply conversing with my mentor. All of a sudden, my children approached us because they were all excited to show me their report cards, which they had just received. I soon found myself negotiating with them on how much their grades were going to cost me—as it is my practice to reward my children for bringing home good grades. After agreeing upon a dollar amount for each letter grade, one particular sister approached me and said, "I would go broke rewarding my children for their good grades." I simply responded by saying, "I do not mind going broke." Stop...

Did anything seem wrong with my response to the sister's comment to me? Yes! My mentor corrected me and said you will not go broke. My statement exposed what I really believed. Even though this situation centered on the grades of my kids and what each of them would get, the truth is that my words revealed my thoughts, and the grades were just a cover up.

What a person truly believes is revealed in those casual moments, when their guard is down.

My mentor had been encouraging church members to be mindful of the things they say and believe. I soon discovered that if I genuinely do not believe a particular thing, then what I do believe would eventually leak from my mouth, usually at the most inappropriate time. I really felt embarrassed because I wanted to look and sound as though I believed the very teaching we had been instructed to follow. In all actuality, I found it difficult to believe the words I was supposed to speak concerning my own life. I was receiving the right information, but I didn't believe that information. I felt that if I simply believed and then rehearsed over and over what I believed, I could eventually change the course of my life. Herein is the main problem…

No one can believe for me or apply change to my life…no one, but me! So who is to blame now? Can I blame my mentor because he's not giving me the right information? Wrong! No wait…what about my church? They're not supporting me. Wrong! Here's the answer. It is God's fault; He's not helping me. Wrong again! I know God has heard them all. The common denominator in each situation is ME! I am the problem. I have to learn to overcome the enemy that is in me.

CHAPTER 4

The Enemy In Me

CHAPTER 4

The Enemy In Me

Now something is wrong here. I have all of the right information. I have a great mentor, great books and reference materials. I also have living examples all around me of individuals who have faced many of life's challenges and have overcome them. But when I look at my own life, I see very little progression. Something is very wrong with this picture. I have all the right information; my pastor's awesome teachings ensure that aspect of my life is covered.

So, where does the problem lie? Why do I continue to take one step forward and two steps back? There has to be something short circuiting my progress.

As I survey my situation and conduct an inspection, I must first start with me. Through this inspection, I discovered that I was subconsciously sabotaging any success or progress I was making. There were a few things that contributed to my unproductive state. The first culprit was fear. Fear has a crippling effect on an individual. It causes one to think illogically. Fear distorts and impairs your sense of judgment. When fear controls a person, it causes the individual to forfeit future opportunities in order to lay claim to present comforts. Because of this, I would dismiss all of the things that God had placed in me. Consequently, I chose to reduce the value I placed on my self-worth, gifts, and talents. What a waste of time and ability.

When fear controls a person, it causes the individual to forfeit future opportunities in order to lay claim to present comforts.

Secret sin in one's life is the other insidious culprit that works to short circuit the progress in a person's life. Though others are unable to see what you do behind closed doors, they can see the effects of your closet behavior. These secret sins eat away at obvious areas of your life and cause them to weaken or decay over time. As Christians, we tend to think that when we asked Jesus to forgive us of our sin that it made us invincible or immune to sin. We have to understand that we are simply forgiven, but the same vulnerability to sin exists within us. And at times, because of this misconception, many Christians think that they are better than sinners, when the truth of the matter is that Christians hide their sins in the dark, while sinners commit their sins in broad daylight. One thing I have learned about sin is that you cannot compartmentalize it. You cannot contain it to one area of your life. It is like a cancer that will spread until it consumes the entire body.

Fear and secret sins are two destructive things that plays a vital role in the short-circuiting of one's success.

Fear and secret sin are two destructive things that play a vital role in the short-circuiting of one's success. If left unchecked, it will wreak havoc in your life. Fear and sin are two of the quickest ways to bring about a quick halt to what God wants to do in your life. It will cause you to forfeit everything you desire to accomplish in life and ultimately send you spiraling out of control to an unfulfilled and unproductive dead end in life.

As I previously stated, the great psalmist, King David, provides us with an appropriate verse of scripture to heed; it reads:

> I have hidden your word in my heart that I might not sin against you.
>
> Psalm 119:11 (NIV)

Hiding the word in your heart will not necessarily prevent you from defying God's word; it will, however, increase the likelihood that you will fulfill God's mandate for your life. This scripture conveys the notion that the more of God's Word you hide in your heart, the greater the possibility that you will not sin. You need the Word to reveal to you where God's boundaries are. However, you must couple your Biblical knowledge with actual application of that Word in order to get the best results of living a dedicated life unto God.

I see a consistent theme throughout the scriptures that underscores the benefits and blessings of obeying God. When we obey God, His blessings then overtake us. On the other hand, I realize that there exists a rather different consequence that we reap whenever we disobey Him. When we choose to wander outside the parameters of God's sovereign will for our lives, we will reap a harvest of curses, non-productivity, lack, as well as a complete void of fulfillment in life.

Read what the book of Deuteronomy has to say about the matter of obeying the will of God:

> If you fully obey the LORD your God and carefully follow all his commands I give you today, the LORD your God will set you high above all the nations on earth. All these blessings will come upon you and accompany you if you obey the LORD your God... However, if you do not obey the LORD your God and do not carefully follow all his commands and decrees I am giving you today, all these curses will come upon you and overtake you:
>
> Deuteronomy 28:1-2, 15 (NIV)

Now I know as a believer, God does not desire for me to be cursed in any way. That said, God doesn't curse me. When I act in disobedience, I trigger the very processes that bring about curses in my own life. My entire family suffers the consequences of my transgressions; the impact does not just affect me alone. The evidence of this fact can be found again in Deuteronomy:

> I call heaven and earth as witnesses today against you, that I have set before you life and death, blessing and cursing; therefore choose life, that both you and your descendants may live;
>
> Deuteronomy 30:19 (NIV)

Who makes the choice, me or God? I am the one who determines which laws are operating in my life, not God. I make that choice when I obey or disobey. It has nothing to do with His love. It has to do with the laws He has ordained in the earth. It is against God's law to bless me while I knowingly operate in disobedience. I don't know your areas of weakness, but I sure know mine.

Stop waiting for deliverance because the Deliverer has already come. The gospel of Luke proclaims:

> The Spirit of the Lord is on me, because he has anointed me to preach good news to the poor. He has sent me to proclaim freedom for the prisoners and recovery of sight for the blind, to release the oppressed,
>
> Luke 4:18 (NIV)

God has already set us free. We do not need to wait for someone else to declare our freedom. You must simply believe it, declare it and walk in it.

> Therefore if any person is [engrafted] in Christ (the Messiah) he is a new creation (a new creature altogether); the old [previous moral and spiritual condition] has passed away. Behold, the fresh and new has come!
>
> 2 Corinthians 5:17 (AMP)

You are already new, and the things that once dominated you no longer have the power to exercise authority over you the way they once did. The power of God and your faith in God's Word have rendered those former things powerless. But any unwillingness to give up the things that jeopardize your future can allow you to remain in a state of captivity.

Although I could skillfully explain it, preach it, and teach it, it used to be a very difficult thing for me to have to walk according to what I was sharing with others. Fear, Low Self Esteem, Lust, Masturbation, and Pornography all held me captive. I was living a hypocritical lifestyle. I would try to stop going to the internet porn sites but kept finding myself back in the same place behind my computer. One of the things that I realized was that when I did well for a month or two, I would think that I could do it on my own, only to be defeated once again. I would forget that I could not keep myself and that it was only through the power of God and my daily trust in Him that I was able to maintain my freedom in Christ.

See, the devil is not interested in scoring a touchdown on the first play of the game. He just wants to keep moving the chains down the field, inch by inch. In others words, Satan knows that he scores touchdowns in our lives whenever we surrender ground to him, no matter how big or small. His objective is simply to make progress or claim more territory for his purposes. Another thing I need to say is that I discovered that my problem with pornography had absolutely nothing to do with my spouse.

Having spoken with individuals who struggle with pornography, I have noticed that once their spouses find out, the innocent ones tend to think that this addiction has something to do with them. That is not the case. The issue resides in the mind of that individual who cannot conquer the images that they have allowed to infiltrate their mind. I had to realize that my addiction was not my wife's fault; it was me. I tried to convince myself that this problem was as a result of what I viewed as a lack of sex in our marriage. I justified my inappropriate behavior by pointing the finger at my wife. Once again, the problem had nothing to do with her. The problem was with me. We tend to make others the scapegoat for our lack of self control or issues we struggle with. Oftentimes, we justify our sins by saying things like, "I was born this way," or "It is because of what my parents did or did not do." At some point, we have to take responsibility for our condition and position in life.

Was living this lie worth it? My future, my

destiny, my marriage and my family were all in jeopardy of being destroyed as a result of my hypocrisy. I had to ask myself whether or not it was more important for me to continue the masquerade or to come clean. I knew that exposing myself meant potential damage to my reputation and embarrassment for me and my loved ones. In the end, I concluded that my relationship with God was more important than continuing to perpetrate a public image that was not real.

I'm learning that the battle must first be conquered in the mind. That's the battleground. If I can win there, I can certainly win my external battles. In the book of Ephesians, the Apostle Paul makes it very plain:

> For we wrestle not against flesh and blood, but against principalities, against powers, against the rulers of the darkness of this world, against spiritual wickedness in high places.
>
> Ephesians 6:12 (KJV)

So, my fight is not a natural fight. I cannot punch the devil in his face. But we must keep in mind that God did not leave us powerless in this fight. He gave us just what we needed to fight back and win! Because the battle is not physical, we cannot wage war with physical weapons. Doing so would be like taking a knife to a gun fight. When we wage spiritual warfare, we must remember…

> For the weapons of our warfare are not physical [weapons of flesh and blood].
>
> 2 Corinthians 10:4a (AMP)

God give me the right tools to do the job. The Message Bible tells me what the weapons are used for:

> We use our powerful God-tools for smashing warped philosophies, tearing down barriers erected against the truth of God, fitting every loose thought and emotion and impulse into the structure of life shaped by Christ. Our tools are ready at hand for clearing the ground of every obstruction and building lives of obedience into maturity."
>
> 2 Corinthians 10:4-6 (MSG)

It is through my knowledge and my obedience that I can now walk in deliverance for real. If I obey all of the instructions of God, I can then activate the laws of blessing in my life. As I stated earlier, the great thing about God is that I am not left defenseless. If I would just submit to God (surrender to his Word and obey it), Resist the devil (trust God to keep me in the time of temptation), he (the enemy) will flee.

PS: Sometimes resisting means that we flee the temptation and simply get away from the computer, television, situation or the person.

CHAPTER 5

Paradigm Shift

CHAPTER 5

Paradigm Shift

Now here I am, not truly happy with my life, and the forecast for the future is not looking too good either. I have a wonderful wife and kids counting on me. I desperately want things to change—as much as anybody in a dire strait does. The real question, therefore, is…am I willing to do what it takes to bring about the change I desire? Am I tired of reading about, hearing about, and seeing other people experiencing all the wonderful things that God has afforded us all? Am I tired of losing when I have already been declared a winner?

It's like being enslaved for 2 years, 5 months, and 18 days and all the while not knowing that you are free. Sounds strange? Well that's what happened to the slaves in Texas. The Emancipation Proclamation, which officially declared the freedom of all slaves, went into effect on January 1, 1863, but the people of Texas (at least the slaves) were not informed until June 19, 1865. I can imagine all of the things that they suffered during this time, things that they did not have to experience, all because they had no clue that they were free.

In much the same way, you and I have many rights. However, we forfeit many of them because we are unaware or we really don't believe that we have been emancipated from certain bondages that have restricted our freedom for so long. Operating in the full liberty that Jesus made possible extends far beyond the basic salvation message.

We really are destroyed or hurt because of what we don't know. In the slaves' case, they had no way of getting the information that declared that they were already free. However, in our case, we tend to simply ignore the information that has already set us free. In my case, this caused me to experience devastating rejection, and it hindered my ability to enjoy the full extent of my liberty in Christ. As a result, my ignorance put my children at a big disadvantage in life.

In the book of Hosea, God warns:

> My people are destroyed from lack of knowledge. "Because you have rejected knowledge, I also reject you as my priests; because you have ignored the law of your God, I also will ignore your children.
> Hosea 4:6 (NIV)

God created you, and He knows what it will take to get you from where you currently are to where you desire to be…and ultimately to where He desires for you to be.

> Isaiah 55:8 (KJV), "for my thoughts are not your thoughts, neither are your ways my ways, saith the LORD".

Pay close attention to the sequence. The reason my ways are not His ways is because my thoughts are not aligned with His thoughts. God knew, as my mentor would say, that your life goes in the direction of your most dominant thought.

> "Their feet run to evil, and they make haste to shed innocent blood: their thoughts are thoughts of iniquity; wasting and destruction are in their paths."
> Isaiah 59:7 (KJV)

Though I may desire to go in another direction, I will ultimately find myself at the destination of my dominant mental paradigms. If there is no path, I will some how create one.

> *"When you control a man's thinking you do not have to worry about his actions. You do not have to tell him not to stand here or go yonder. He will find his 'proper place' and will stay in it. You do not need to send him to the back door. He will go without being told. In fact, if there is no back door, he will cut one for his special benefit. His education makes it necessary."*
>
> –Carter G. Woodson

I don't believe that God wants my thoughts and ways to remain contrary to His thoughts and ways. Therefore, He has provided a way for me to align myself with Him, so I can see things His way. The fear of the LORD really is the beginning of knowledge, according to Proverbs 1:7.

Though many great men down through the years have discovered awesome wonders, they can never declare that they were the originators of anything because it all starts and ends with God. God knew that certain things had to be in place in order for His way of thinking to become my thinking or paradigm.

What are paradigms? The word paradigm comes from the Greek word paradeigma, which which means "pattern" or "example." Merriam-Webster's dictionary defines paradigms as a set of assumptions, concepts, values, and practices that constitutes a way of viewing reality. As I began to research the meaning of a paradigm, I found something very interesting. According to M. L. Handa, a professor of sociology who first introduced the idea of social paradigm; in order for a system of thought to become an accepted dominate paradigm certain conditions must be in place to facilitate this shift.

Seven Conditions That Facilitate a Paradigm Shift

M.L. Handa (Secular)	**Christian**
Professional organizations that give legitimacy to the paradigm.	The Church
Dynamic leaders and Educators who introduce and support the paradigm.	"...Apostles; and some, prophets; and some, evangelists; and some, pastors and teachers." **Eph 4:11**
Journalists and editors who write about the system of thought. They both disseminate the information essential to the paradigm and give the paradigm legitimacy.	The Bible which has about 40 different writers.
Government agencies who give credence to the paradigm.	The Kingdom of God
Conferences are conducted that are devoted to discussing ideas central to the paradigm.	Christian Conferences are conducted throughout the Body of Christ. (Annually, Semi-annually)
Media coverage	TBN, Daystar, WHT, JOLTV.com
Sources of funding to further research on the paradigm.	Tithes and Offerings

All these things are in place to aide us in making a change from one way of thinking to another. It's a revolution, a transformation. In writing to the Christians in Rome, the Apostle Paul declared:

> Do not be conformed to this world (this age), [fashioned after and adapted to its external, superficial customs], but be transformed (changed) by the [entire] renewal of your mind [by its new ideals and its new attitude], so that you may prove [for yourselves] what is the good and acceptable and perfect will of God, even the thing which is good and acceptable and perfect [in His sight for you].
>
> Romans 12:2 (AMP)

I cannot possibly prove, examine, or rightly divide the will or Word of God correctly if I first have not had a change of mind or paradigm shift.

God knows what I need in order to shift my thinking so that I can think correctly about who I am in Christ and about all the things that my relationship with Him has afforded me. God has given me everything I need in order to operate in this life successfully, and He has also provided what I need in order to secure my eternity.

> As His divine power has given to us all things that pertain to life and godliness, through the knowledge of Him who called us by glory and virtue,
>
> 2 Peter 1:3 (NKJV)

So now what am I going to do? All of my excuses have been eliminated. All of the chains have been loosened. There is nothing left to stop me, but me.

One thing I have learned is that you cannot give reliable directions to a place you have never been. Even with Mapquest, someone had to first chart the course to ensure that you will get accurate directions to your destination. I can remember once giving directions to a group of people, only to discover later that the information I gave them was wrong. Many times we find ourselves getting bad directions that end up costing us precious time, energy and money. God has very specific and highly reliable directions, or should I say plans, for us already mapped out for our individual journeys in life.

God's directions are always precise because He has already been where you are going...

A favorite scripture of mine out of Jeremiah assures us that God has a definite plan for each of our lives:

> For I know the plans I have for you," declares the LORD, "plans to prosper you and not to harm you, plans to give you hope and a future".
>
> Jeremiah 29:11 (NIV)

God's directions are always precise because He has already been where you are going, and He has already mapped out your journey based upon some very fixed reference points. God tells us in:

> Isaiah 46:10 "Declaring the end from the beginning and from ancient times the things that are not yet done, saying, My counsel shall stand, and I will do all My pleasure." This lets me know that I can trust His directions.

On the other hand, my wife places no confidence in my ability to get the family from point A to point B whenever we take a family trip. She second-guesses me every step of the way. According to my wife, my directions are never that good. To be quite honest, I can't say that I blame her all that much, given the fact that I often second-guess my own navigational abilities on the open road. BUT! God's directions are always accurate and highly reliable. He has a certain knack for getting us to our exact destination, oftentimes, without us ever realizing the turns and detours He causes us to take. So trust His leading.

CHAPTER 6

A Piece of the Puzzle

CHAPTER 6

A Piece of the Puzzle

It wasn't until November of 2006 that I really started to understand that I was very important to God and that my life really does matter. During this time, I began to see just how much God values you and I. God cared for us so much that He gave His best gift to secure our future. You have to value yourself just as much as God does. Your life is very precious, and you must see it that way. My pastor often says that we may not have been worthy of the sacrifice Jesus made on our behalf, but we were definitely worth it. To God, we were and are worth the sacrifice of His dear Son.

I saw a puzzle of Mickey Mouse in a frame at the house of some family friends. It drew my attention because within each puzzle piece, there were images of other Disney characters. Yet each of the pieces, when put together reflected the complete image of Mickey Mouse. Now I know this seems funny and I didn't think much of it at the time, but later on that month, it would help me see something about myself. God showed me that I was neither the puzzle nor the picture. Instead, I was an integral piece of the entire puzzle. And when all the important pieces come together, they form a beautiful mosaic that we can all appreciate.

Now, what did that help me to understand? Well...just like the puzzle, the Body of Christ is made up of many pieces, or parts as the Apostle Paul states in the book of 1 Corinthians.

> The body is a unit, though it is made up of many parts; and though all its parts are many, they form one body. So it is with Christ.
>
> 1 Corinthians 12:12 (NIV)

No one piece is greater than the others. But each piece is necessary in order for the puzzle to be complete. Now this alleviated a lot of pressure, but it also showed me that I am part of something great, a reality that greatly elevated my self-worth. Consider how the Message Bible conveys this exact point:

> I want you to think about how all this makes you more significant, not less. A body isn't just a single part blown up into something huge. It's all the different-but-similar parts arranged and functioning together.
>
> 1 Corinthians 12:14 (MSG)

I don't have to try to do it all or be it all. My responsibility and focus should be on my piece or my part, so that the overall puzzle can be complete. Furthermore, each piece has its specific place. No other piece can be inserted into a place that is designed for one particular piece. No matter how hard we try, it cannot be forced into the position it was not designed to fill, and the puzzle is still not complete as long as this wandering piece is out of position—despite how well the other pieces have found their niche.

No one piece is greater than the others. But each piece is necessary in order for the puzzle to be complete.

God has a plan, and I am part of it. It does not matter how much more talented and gifted another person is; they cannot take your place. It matters not how articulate they are because there is a designated place for you. So what are you waiting on? Get up and take your place in God!

On January 8, 1976, God saw fit to write me into History or His Story, as I prefer to say. I was not born in another time and place. God knew exactly when and where to place me in order to fulfill the specific plan He designed just for me. Just to reiterate the fact that God has you in mind, let's revisit what the prophet Jeremiah declared to the people:

> For I know the plans I have for you," declares the LORD, "plans to prosper you and not to harm you, plans to give you hope and a future.
>
> Jeremiah 29:11 (NIV)

God gave a vision to my mentor, and that plan included me, one important piece of the puzzle. The year God gave him the plan, I was a toddler in Philadelphia. There, I grew to be a foolish young man; nevertheless, God had a purpose for me inside the plan He gave to my mentor. But in order for the plan or puzzle to be completed, destiny would have to ensure that my piece made its way into proper position. My mentor is from Chicago, IL, and I am from Philadelphia, PA. Therefore, God had to maneuver my life (one piece of the puzzle) to end up inside the vision that God gave to the man whom God uses to mentor my life. This individual has the awesome responsibility of putting the puzzle together, once the various pieces come under his care and authority. During one particular dinner for ministers and their wives, I saw something that captured my attention. I simply marveled at how God had brought many pieces from various areas and diverse walks of life to one place—noting how we are being assembled just like puzzle pieces in order to reflect the very image that is on the puzzle box. We are being assembled so that we would reflect to the world the image of the Lord Jesus Christ.

In writing to the Roman Christians, the Apostle Paul said it like this:

> For those God foreknew he also predestined to be conformed to the likeness of his Son, that he might be the firstborn among many brothers.
>
> Romans 8:29 (NIV)

We are assembled to reflect the image of the Son, not our own image. I recall that when I looked closely at each piece of the Mickey Mouse puzzle, each piece had its own distinct shape and image. But each image, on each of the individual pieces, came together to reflect the overall picture on the box. My part is not someone else's part, and someone else's part is not mine. But each part, when it is perfectly assembled, reflects a glorious image to the beholder. This realization of how various puzzle pieces can come together to form a distinct picture is what helped me to know that I am a valuable part of God's overall plan in this day and age. Today, I know for sure that I am where God wants me to be, at the exact time He wanted me to be here.

In sharing the importance of pursuing purpose and destiny, Mordecai admonished his cousin, Esther, by stating:

> And who knows but that you have come to the kingdom for such a time as this and for this very occasion?
>
> Esther 4:14b (AMP)

The great thing about God is that He doesn't hold my past failures against me. Each day that I wake up, I have another opportunity to change my tomorrows by the decisions I make today. We should take great comfort in the encouraging words found in the book of Lamentations:

> Through the LORD's mercies we are not consumed, Because His compassions fail not. They are new every morning; Great is Your faithfulness.
>
> Lamentations 3:22-23 (NKJV)

This is great news because everyday you wake up, you have another opportunity to reformat your future. Everyday you have a chance to change your tomorrow. If you do not like the course your life is taking, the power is in your hand to chart a new course with a more promising destination. You can make the right decisions today that will improve the future for you, your family and everyone else connected to you.

If you do not like the course your life is taking, the power is in your hand to chart a new course with a more promising destination.

People have a tendency to try and remind you of who and what you used to be. They may even remember you based on what you used to do, but God chooses not to retain those negative images from our pasts. The past is the past; so let it pass. The writer of the 103rd Psalm states:

> As far as the east is from the west, so far hath he removed our transgressions from us.
>
> Psalm 103:12 (KJV)

The prophet Jeremiah declared God's views of forgiveness in this manner:

> And they shall teach no more every man his

> neighbour, and every man his brother, saying, Know the LORD: for they shall all know me, from the least of them unto the greatest of them, saith the LORD: for I will forgive their iniquity, and I will remember their sin no more.
>
> Jeremiah 31:34 (KJV)

I'm not at a disadvantage. God has forgiven me, and I have forgiven myself. According to that famous line from the movie, ***Shawshank Redemption***..."*It is time to get busy livin' or get busy dyin.*"

I chose to get busy living. I chose the life that Jesus bled and died to give me. Yes, I have made many mistakes, and I have made many bad decisions. However, I cannot afford to waste another day of my life having a pity party. We all have fallen short in many areas, but we do not have to remain there, and we certainly do not have to continue to make the same bad choices.

> Romans 3:23 says, "For all have sinned, and come short of the glory of God."

Now, when I say I am ready to get busy livin', I simply mean that I must be willing to go through certain trials and do what is necessary for me to live the life that Jesus' death makes possible. You must do all that is necessary to make your dreams a reality. When I was growing up, we use to say, "I'm going for broke." The expression meant that we were going to do everything we knew to do in order to get whatever we wanted. We would forget about fear and what other people would say concerning our choices. Nothing would stop us from reaching our goals.

I saw nothing wrong with that statement until my mom and 1st Lady of our ministry asked me "why do you have to go for broke?" Stop and think about it! After doing everything that I knew to do and after giving my all, I would simply end up right where I confessed—broke. Not just broke financially but also broken and damaged emotionally because of unfulfilled expectation. "Why can't you go for increase," she said. Stop and think about it. If I'm careful, and I do all that God instructs me to do, I would ultimately find myself in a place of abundant increase—the place that God desires for me and the place I desire for myself. By meditating on God's word, I would have made my way prosperous, instead.

You must do all that is necessary to make your dream a reality.

Today, I choose to go for increase, rather than for broke. I have determined to pursue life in all its fullness. What about you? In the book of Deuteronomy, God commanded the children of Israel to decide whether to follow life or death:

> This day I call heaven and earth as witnesses against you that I have set before you life and death, blessings and curses. Now choose life, so that you and your children may live.
>
> Deuteronomy 30:19 (NIV)

Hopefully, you will decide to pursue life, as well. If so, then put this book down and get busy livin' the life you have been afforded. The world is waiting for us. To ensure that you get maximum results for your efforts, follow the steps below:

1. Get the right information (God's Word).

Isaiah 48:17b "I am the LORD thy God which teacheth thee to profit, which leadeth thee by the way that thou shouldest go."

2. Believe it wholeheartedly.

Proverbs 23:7 "For as he thinketh in his heart, so is he."

3. Allow it to dominate your thinking.

Philippians 2:5 "Let this mind be in you, which was also in Christ Jesus."

4. Last and most importantly...get up and DO SOMETHING!

> Psalm 1:3 "and he shall be like a tree planted by the rivers of water, that bringeth forth his fruit in his season; his leaf also shall not wither; and whatsoever he doeth shall prosper."

GO FOR INCREASE!

CHAPTER 7

Appreciation for the Process

CHAPTER 7

Appreciation for the Process

I recall times when my mentor would take me and a few other brothers to see his new house, during various stages of construction. We got an opportunity to walk on the concrete foundation and see the workers erect the wood frame. He took us on guided tours of his house, describing the various features as though it had been completed. I would smile and listen, but I never really found it interesting. Somehow, I believe he knew that, but he continued to take me out there anyway.

In all honesty, I was only truly interested in the finished product. Though, I had no idea that my lack of interest with that whole building process spoke volumes about me. He would often say that everything you do—from how you drive, to how you dress—says something about how you see yourself and your approach to life.

I did not understand the wisdom of his words then, but I certainly do now. As it is with the building process—from the breaking of the ground, to the laying of the concrete, to the building of the frame—successful lives are established by following a methodical process.

Turning an architect's conceptual drawings into a completed house mirrors the way our lives are established. The blueprint for our lives resides in our minds, but we must go through a systematic process to pull what we see in the mind out onto the real world canvas. Our mental blueprints exist in the form of dreams, which must one day find their foundation in reality. In the process of building dreams, however, you and I are guaranteed to encounter difficult obstacles and challenges.

Our mental blueprints exist in the form of dreams, which must one day find their foundation in reality.

You will have to deal with a variety of emotions, as well as confront many of your greatest fears and insecurities. But this is all a necessary part of the process. With every process that forges great things, there are always many valleys, twists and turns, distractions, discouragements, and delays. These things come to test your resolve and desire to pursue the prize.

God created the entire universe, the heavens and earth, in just six days. But everything after that miraculous construction project has to go through the natural unfolding process of time in order to come into existence. Everything must start in its infancy. We must be willing to begin at this point and then progress to further stages of development. We cannot afford to bypass any of the critical steps in the growth process. Every stage of your development serves to increase your capacity to withstand the challenges that can threaten your future success. In trying to rebuke and encourage Job, Bildad stated to his friend:

> Your beginnings will seem humble, so prosperous will your future be.
>
> Job 8:7 (NIV)

The book of Zechariah offers hope to anyone who has ever envisioned a big dream but felt hindered by too few resources to do anything with their dream:

> Do not despise these small beginnings, for the Lord rejoices to see the work begin,
>
> Zechariah 4:10 (NLT)

One morning, I found myself walking through a new housing development area. The contractors were putting the finishing touches on many of the houses. As I walked past one of the houses where they were finishing the driveway, I could tell something was wrong. Now, I don't claim to be an expert in the field of housing construction, but I knew enough to know that the worker was skipping critical steps in the construction of that driveway.

He did not include the all-important steel reinforcement (commonly referred to as "rebar") that serves to provide structural strength to the concrete after it hardens—allowing it to withstand the weight of heavy static and dynamic loads, such as parked and moving vehicles. Additionally, the rebar is used to minimize cracking to the concrete surface. The steel reinforcement won't prevent cracks altogether, but it will help hold the surface together if they do form. That worker also failed to incorporate control joints to help prevent and/or contain random cracking. This young man's lack of attention to detail or willful disregard for city building codes is certain to cost the unfortunate home owner thousand of dollars in repair costs.

Not too long ago, my home suffered some very bad hail damage. All said and done, the storm ended up costing me over sixteen thousand dollars worth of interior and exterior damage. The house sustained many holes to the roof, which eventually led to some very serious water damage. To remedy the problem, I hired a roofing company to repair the roof, giving them half of the money up front to get started.

To begin the work, the roofer would need to secure a city permit, authorizing him to do work of this nature. Once completed, the roofer would have to undergo a city inspection to ensure the quality of his work according to city building codes. And once the contractor passes the final city inspection, I would then release to him the remaining balance of the contract. However…

I was unaware of the scheduled time of the final city inspection. Mind you, our house has upper and lower level roofing that needed to be repaired. When I came home one day, to my utter surprise, I ran into the city inspector who informed me that he had just completed the roof inspection.

When I began to question the inspector regarding the status of his inspection, he informed me that the roof had passed and met with his approval. After thanking the inspector for his integrity and honesty, because of my concern for the quality of the roofer's workmanship, I noticed that his countenance changed very suddenly. He informed me rather reluctantly that he was not being honest with me, at all. He said, "I want to be straight with you. I did not check the upper level. But the company has a good reputation." Now you can imagine my shock and anger at hearing this.

Because of the willful disregard for the performance of his official duties, this gross dereliction of duty could have potentially cost me thousands of dollars more somewhere down the line. The main point here is that you cannot afford to skip crucial steps in the building stages of your life, or risk the possibility of compromising the integrity of the finished product, thus decreasing the value of what you are building.

I believe everyone desires to be successful. When teachers ask their students, "What do you want to do when you grow up?" I do not believe any child ever says, "When I grow up, I want to be a failure. I do not want to see any of my dreams come to pass, and I want to have a life that is unfulfilling." No one wants that type of life. No one goes into a marriage saying that they desire to have their marriage fail miserably or that they want to be damaged emotionally in the process. But if we do not do what is necessary to have a successful marriage then failure will be the outcome, despite our desires to the contrary. We may have the desire to be successful, and we may possess the potential to fulfill every desire we have, but the question remains... Are you willing to do what is necessary to obtain success and realize your full potential?

According to the Word of God, we can all enjoy the good that this earth has to offer:

> If you are willing and obedient, you will eat the best from the land;
>
> Isaiah 1:19 (NIV)

You may be willing to eat the best that this world has to offer, but if you are not also willing to do what it takes to obtain the best things in life, then you will live and die with that desire unfilled. I said this earlier, but this is a great place to restate this thought. We all come to planet earth with an assignment to fulfill; and only in that assignment will you find your greatest joy fulfilled. We also come full of potential and pregnant with possibility. But it is our

We all come to earth with an assignment to fulfill, and only in that assignment will you find your greatest joy fulfilled.

willingness to submit to certain processes that determine if our potential is ever maximized and whether our possibilities are ever realized.

My mentor says often that perseverance will always outlast persecution. It is the difference between winning and losing. The one who perseveres and maintains a single-minded focus on purpose will have too much invested to ever give up. Change is inevitable, and positive change typically spells out an arduous and tedious journey. Nevertheless, it is the only road that everyone must travel in order to move from your current station in life to where you desire to be.

It never ceases to amaze me just how funny life is at times. By observing the process of home construction, I have gained a true appreciation for the process involved in changing mere dreamers into truly great individuals. Go figure…

Footprints to Freedom

CHAPTER 1

Conquering Yourself

You must learn to conquer the very things that threaten your purpose and dreams.

Owning up to our past failures does not mean that we allow them to become crutches or excuses.

Whoever bears the responsibility also possesses the authority to make the necessary changes.

CHAPTER 2

The Masquerade

Reality is based on perception.

Your mentor is not the one who gives you the instruction you need. He or she is the one whose instructions you take and apply to your life.

...it is very difficult to assess yourself worth correctly without knowing who you are.

CHAPTER 3

A Change of Heart

The information you receive is what affects your decision-making, which determines your actions and ultimately the entire course of your life.

What a person truly believes is revealed in those casual moments, when their guard is down.

CHAPTER 4

The Enemy in Me

When fear controls a person, it causes the individual to forfeit future opportunities in order to lay claim to persent comfort.

Fear and secret sins are two destructive things that play a vital role in the short-circuiting of ones success.

CHAPTER 5

Paradigm Shift

God's directions are always precise because He has already been where you are going...

CHAPTER 6

A Piece of the Puzzle

No one piece is greater that the others. But each piece is necessary in order for the puzzle to be complete.

If you do not like the course your life is taking, the power is in your hand to chart a new course with a more promising destination.

CHAPTER 7

Appreciation for the Process

Our mental blueprints exist in the form of dreams, which must one day find their foundation in reality.

We all come to planet earth with an assignment to fulfill; and only in that assignment will you find your greatest joy fulfilled.

Notes

Notes

About the Author

Charles J Bennett III is an author, spiritual leader, and mentor who has inspired, imparted, and impacted the lives of individuals from various spiritual, social, and economic backgrounds. He has traveled throughout the United States as well as Japan and the Republic of Korea. He currently lives in El Paso, TX with his wife, Talisha and four children.

CPSIA information can be obtained
at www.ICGtesting.com
Printed in the USA
FSOW01n1251260716
22973FS